ACCIDENTS
AFTER
HAPPENING

ACCIDENTS AFTER HAPPENING

POEMS

ROBERT PRIEST

Copyright © Robert Priest, 2025

Published by ECW Press
665 Gerrard Street East
Toronto, Ontario, Canada M4M 1Y2
416-694-3348 / info@ecwpress.com

All rights reserved. No part of this publication may be reproduced, stored in a retrieval system, or transmitted in any form by any process — electronic, mechanical, photocopying, recording, or otherwise — without the prior written permission of the copyright owners and ECW Press. The scanning, uploading, and distribution of this book via the internet or via any other means without the permission of the publisher is illegal and punishable by law. This book may not be used for text and data mining, AI training, and similar technologies. Please purchase only authorized electronic editions, and do not participate in or encourage electronic piracy of copyrighted materials. Your support of the author's rights is appreciated.

Editor for the Press: Michael Holmes /
a misFit Book
Copy editor: Shannon Parr
Cover image: CSA Images / iStock
Cover design: Jess Albert

LIBRARY AND ARCHIVES CANADA CATALOGUING IN PUBLICATION

Title: Accidents after happening : poems / Robert Priest.

Names: Priest, Robert, 1951- author

Identifiers: Canadiana (print) 20250223221X | Canadiana (ebook) 20250223244

ISBN 978-1-77041-853-0 (softcover)
ISBN 978-1-77852-507-0 (PDF)
ISBN 978-1-77852-506-3 (ePub)

Subjects: LCGFT: Poetry.

Classification: LCC PS8581.R47 A64 2025 | DDC C811/.54—dc23

This book is funded in part by the Government of Canada. *Ce livre est financé en partie par le gouvernement du Canada.* We acknowledge the support of the Canada Council for the Arts. *Nous remercions le Conseil des arts du Canada de son soutien.* We would like to acknowledge the funding support of the Ontario Arts Council (OAC) and the Government of Ontario for their support. We also acknowledge the support of the Government of Ontario through the Ontario Book Publishing Tax Credit, and through Ontario Creates.

PRINTED AND BOUND IN CANADA

PRINTING: COACH HOUSE   5 4 3 2 1

To Marsha Lee Kirzner

Contents

More Than Never	1
To What Is Us	2
I Took a Word	3
Our Love May Be Infinite	5
Physics of Osculation	6
Love for the Hell of It	7
Micropoems I	9
White Man	11
Seventy	14
Lust	17
In Fuck-Love	19
Black Brogues	21
Pain at the Back of the Eyes	25
A Dead Bit	26
Picture of My Father	28
Oarsman	33
The Yellow House	36
The Day After the End of the World	38
Micropoems II	39
Swipe	40
The Side I'm On	42
Hunger from a Drone	46
Curse on a Warmonger	47
Hate Takes You Back	48
Insurrection Day	49
We Burn More People	50
Twelve Things I Learned from My Research	51
What Happened to the Ark	52
The Promise of Peace	53
Micropoems III	55
It Won't Fit into Poetry	56

Poetry Expects	57
For Your Eyes Only	59
Clock at Midnight	60
Apple	62
Potato	64
Inside the Onion	65
Papaya	66
The Weed That Grows Wild	67
Micropoems IV	70
If All Words Were Rose	71
Key	72
Guitar Heroics	73
Prince Pantoum	75
Because I Don't Forgive Brown Sugar or Some Girls	76
Micropoems V	77
A Where Ness	79
Mr. Joe	80
Where Is Peter	82
The Neighbourhood Is Not the Same	84
Elegy for Masami	85
Many Elegies	87
Space Where Michael Was	89
One Hundred Thousand Poets	91
Always Almost	94
Micropoems VI	96
Go Get a Parachute and Fall	97
Let's Not Wait	98
To Make It Happen	100
Rash Wish	102
When We Make Love	103
A Just Love	105
I Love You Now	107
I Believe	109
So Much Distance	110

Micropoems VII	112
Baby Steps	114
Granddaughter	117
Halfway	120
Acknowledgements	123

More Than Never

We may not be one
awareness

but we share
a hinge

We all swing
into the same frame

doors
to one interior

How often with a single touch
do we all open at once?

More than never
Possibly as often as always

To What Is Us

The roads not taken
branch out

from the centre
of every footfall

Roads well hidden
Roads into old-growth timber

Roads back to lovers
who do not wait

Infinite intersections
cross our hearts

Every step
a nexus

to what is us
just beyond the horizon

Always
right here

at the vanishing
point

I Took a Word

I took a word
from a word
and the word
was still full of words
so I took another
and another
and just when I thought
I might have too many
I realized that every word I'd taken
was full of other words

I could describe the universe
twice
I could beg forever and never repeat myself
There was enough there for poetry
for mathematics
I could make mistakes
go off on tangents
always on overflow
and yet
the language seemed
to have a pulse
One minute it was
like I was buried alive
in words beyond control
and the next
I'd look at you
and in one breath
suck them all back in
to the original
solemn word

I took
from the first word
and say nothing

Our Love May Be Infinite

Our love
may be infinite

but it fits here
my lips against yours

teetering into each other
eyes full of only *now*

the sharpness of each sensation
widening the moment

making room for
making time for

breath after breath
just to hold each other here

we can't help
but make a time and place

for the whole Earth
and all the stars and dark matters

Physics of Osculation

When we travel, life slows down
Different people see us differently
It depends on how still our love is

If our love is deeply moving
then a kiss can take forever — to begin
And once it does it is possible
that there is neither time nor place

When tongues touch
we are close to telepathy
Which is why a kiss is slow
because it has so much information
to get out and in simultaneously

What if we were to travel
on a kiss at light speed
and look back?
How would your face look?
How would my face look?

Would there still be any distance
between the two of us at all?

Love for the Hell of It

Love for the hell of it
for the dirty dishes
and the misunderstanding
for the insult and the quarrels
Love knowing that approval
and disdain are inseparable
Love for the thrown cup
and the word *cunt*
under the breath hurting the throat

Love for the shot at improvement
and the certainty of going down
for the never answered
and the constantly repeated
for arriving again and again and again
at your anger
the apology given and not received
for time crawling and time slipping
for the knitting and the rending
Love for the instant that becomes the long haul

out of fear, out of divine longing
catching glints of ecstasy
trapped in despair
for the best in you being brought out
by the worst of times
Love for the injustice and the ease
for deep space separations and claustrophobic closeness
for the taste of tongue and the scent of madness
Love for the earth of it
for the river of it

for tenderness at any second
right out of yourself and into the other
to lose and not mind
to give, to understand
and at last, to empathize
to get your dick in
to get your heart in
to throw your heart against the wall
with bitter words instantly regretted
going through the regret beyond regret
forgiven and forgiving
for something not self

Micropoems I

That constant ringing — it's the alarm going off for now or never

Evil doesn't see evil in itself, only in others

In a fight to the death, who's right depends on who's left

It's evil versus evil — pick a side

You can't point to everything at once

War criminals calling war criminals war criminals

No one wants to be questioned but everyone wants to be answered

No one expects the American Inquisition

If the right is wrong is the left right? Hup, hup

When a butcher enters a palace, the butcher doesn't become a king,
    the palace becomes an abattoir
(after an existing Turkish proverb)

Love for one's enemy is most often unrequited

One just makes triggers
another just makes barrels
a whole child explodes

Apocalypse is personal

That undertone of worldwide screaming is just the sound of victors writing history

Who makes the weapons makes the wars

When a democracy dies it turns into a corps

Sure there's a hole, but it's in the other end of the boat

There is very little weeping among war profiteers

The last thing keeping a sinking ship afloat is the frantic paddling of the rats who were too afraid to desert

Peace won't make itself

Peace is the great philanthropy

May the children of war be the parents of peace

if it's not a peace for all

it's not peace at all

White Man

My hair as a child was so sun-bleached
even white people called me *whitey*

But looking in the mirror I always thought
I had rainbow possibilities

The birthmark on my arm
is chestnut brown

and I have multiple melanin specks
little smudges of brown

all over me
I'm freckled

flecked with scalloped circles of maroon
I have beet-red bits

Elsewhere I'm chicken-like
not really white so much as pallid

I could easily pass for pasty
for part of the moon

but I have purple veins in my neck
and a blue scar on my inner lip

where a dentist drilled me
a screaming new amalgam tattoo

My eyes vary — lapis here
lazuli there

but other hues compete
are my pupils black, grey, brown?

Subdued but coursing
on the back of my hands, indigo veins meander

There is no accurate single vocable
for the tint of my areolas, my nipples

Even their shades
have shades

My tongue might be generalized as pink-*ish*
but what a stippled rubescent purple-pink it sometimes is

so different from the violet of my lips
the thin grey of my goatee and silvering hair

Mollusc-tinged
my glans penis is never the same hue twice

and inside I'm told
my organs are a motley palette

with cerulean streamers
My blood is blue or red, always changing

A browny beige star
atop my taint

Come close and you'll see me full spectrum
I'm a regular Josef's coat

a screwed up painter's rag
a butterfly wing

But only till a siren sounds
That's when I draw away from the mirror

just far enough to let the rainbow blur back
into its safe white monotone

Seventy

The ageing continues
or, worse, it doesn't
You think young
but the pops and cracks
of knees and neck
penetrate the mind
Those rivers of magic thought
ride a new template now
thin-branching spider veins

The dancing you still want to do
can no longer invulnerably
toss long locks
or twerk the hips
without a week to recover
No matter how bad the eyes get
the lines in your face deepen

You are still good at watching TV
Your excellence in appreciating
the beauty of the other
seems immortal
But the body you bared
in careless glory
now sports blots and spots

where time spills its coffee
on your fresh white pages

No need to shave those legs
time has rubbed them smooth

and shiny
The phallus
once so ever ready
to pop its hat
and bare the vertical grin
is rarely summoned now
more a rumple than a stiltskin

Just as the larynx drops its register
a couple of rungs
the plans and blueprints for new works
multiply magically
Your mind is better than it ever was
but ageing is never like
winter in retreat
it only goes deeper into winter
until it doesn't

The creased sheet of skin
the catacombed bones
the flecked embedding of
eternal eyes

There's no cursor in the palm
to indicate just where you are
in the lifeline
so you consider your blessings
You catalogue your works
you scour your past
glad for what you no longer are
but scared for what you may soon be

Those moments so far off
they might as well be never

are coming up
Time spent disbelieving will only use up
that much more of the little left
Your complex chemistry
your particles, your waves
everything that is not you about you
will disperse

Once so distant
it didn't matter
something called death
is already eyeing your remaining ink
its bony finger
eager for the keyboard
keen to close the bracket
and end the sentence
with one last
black dot

Lust

It stops in its tracks and stares like a dog
no more manners than a compass needle
Propriety has not informed
its sudden fattening
its jolly thickness
It swells the tongue and licks the lips
all our serious talk
mere lubrication
for the old in and out
We are bonobos, fuck monsters
If we could see what sudden kicks
we all get from incorrect thoughts
we'd have to recalibrate
the onset and enunciation
of mutual cancellation
We are not righteous, we are not ascetic
Lust licks up the legs
with long fire-fattening flames
Suddenly we are wet
incorrectly
Lust only knows
the other end of the rose
It shrinks the world to a little accidental up-skirt
and has no end of resurrections
The bow springs back, the tendon twangs
the arrow is nose, is tongue
The deeper decorum goes
lust just licks under it
and there's no depth deep enough
Open lust's octagon
and there are octagons within

for lust to press onward and into
It peoples the cells with starseed, specks the flesh
with every word but *wait*
Its dictionary is all *please*
and *more* and *more*
and the words *stop* and *not*
vanish from its pulsing pages
glad for the kink-tip of twinkle
upright in the stardust
of the eyes

Pleased to think
that no one hears the galloping
we ride the nose-thick bronco
into the well of lust
down the well
one horse after another
the buffalo screaming, stampeding
tumbling, falling

In Fuck-Love

I feel it coming from far away
the thought of fuck
All the synonyms for fuck
rush through some small channel in my throat
Three, four, and five words at a time
busting me open
The word replicates
faster than it can be redacted

I take every road to fuck you
I am only half a fuck without you
It takes two tongues to utter
our one-word vocabulary
We are only everything
that is necessary
for total and complete utterly fulfilling fucking
with nothing left over
fingers, lips — mere fuck functions
the brain but a fuck organ
Fuck is our marriage vow
It is the ever-varying locked-on-repeat sacred
We are god's fuck engine
our bodies clasped together
in fuck prayer
flames fused in holy fuck fire

We are never not fucking
We are either on our way to
or already deep in
the ease
the languor

the friction
of fuck-lagration
We are fuck animals
in forever fuck
fucking ourselves silly
sleep-fucking
dream-fucking
We wake up fuck-walking
fuck singing
I can't fuck for myself
unless I fuck for you
Fuck away my bones
Fuck the dust out of me
Fuck like the world depends on it
joy-fucking
in fuck-love
till we are both so
truly duly fully fucked raw
there is nothing left to do
but pause
and pant
a little while
before we fuck again
our groins groaning all baritone
this other word for *thank you*
this other word for *yes*

Black Brogues

Unsafe black plastic shoes
imitation brogues
bought very cheap but a perfect fit
Unsafe because
the soles are smooth
gripless
Too easy to slip and wrench your back
with a sudden jerking recovery move
arms askew
like a fool on a banana peel
crack your head open
in a complete up-ender

but the only shoes I could bear
to wear
when I felt most unsafe
Fourteen months
in a psych ward
terrified of the idea
of spending money
scared to drain away
the little
I dreamed I had left

So I trod cautiously
when my friends came
on a daily basis
to walk me
outside
hyperaware

of super smooth surfaces
patches of ice

Everything was dangerous
anyway
The dust I am
hardly clinging together

My own weight
my skin
thinning away
My skeleton
gaining more and more definition

It took fourteen high-voltage
electroshock sessions
to bring me around
So in the moment
I had no past
Each day the amnesia asking
Really, I've been in here for 14 months?
Really?

I returned home finally in those plastic shoes
still terrified to buy a better pair
Terrified to walk more than a block or two
seeing portents in the clouds
catastrophe everywhere imminent

Three years later
well-shod in expensive Campers
Bob the guitar player bought me
those old plastic brogues
half forgotten

are shoved face forward
into a slot in the well-populated shoe shelf

Sometimes reaching for my new shoes
I grab the backs of the old ones
by mistake
and pulling them out
shudder at the sight
and shove them back
superstitious
remembering fragments
of wintry sidewalks
I'd trudged shakily
someone holding my elbow
trying to joke me out of madness
reason me out of psychosis

Today, two pairs of shoes later
looking for something to wear
while I painted the front door
I took them out deliberately
covered with a thin grey film
of dust but otherwise
workable
walkable
But I shake my head
Not for the dirtiest task on Earth
could I be convinced to slip my feet
back into these haunted hollows

I have an urge to put them out
free for the taking
but I pause
Would that be fair?

Did my sickness imbue them
with a curse?
Would it go off walking
with their unknowing new owner?

Just throwing them away though
wasting them
when people went unshod in the world
also troubled me

I take a deep breath, dangling them by the heels
in front of the unit
karma ridden
two cast-off shadow feet

Shuddering
I push them back
into their dark slot

Pain at the Back of the Eyes

Pain
spills the medium
a vein full
of too many veins

There aren't enough
alphabets
The codes are blown
It is more than information
can stand

It gathers at the temples
pits the jawbones
pushes in at the ears

There is nowhere in the body
big enough for this
scream

A Dead Bit

I thought we had a word together
but obviously not
We were just speaking
I gave you the word
but nothing came back
I lost a word
I could have given to the wind
or the river
for all the sense it made
and yet I was walking around
magnetized
held in place by this
word I thought
we'd had
I reached the stretched outer edge
of my ambit
I found a sharper perimeter
to the meaning
Of course I hung on
to nothing

I was flung
centrifugally
but no one told me
I thought stars
were naturally smeared
I thought we had gravity
I thought we had physics together
but I guess that was
my own chatter coming back

That was just me
listening to me
and you staring blankly off
like a dead bit of sky

Picture of My Father

He began as a photograph
on the dresser
a man at sea
the white circle of a sailor's cap
like a halo 'round his head
the face handsome, proud

Another shot has him sitting in a swivel seat
at the back end of a mile-long cannon
aimed at the sky
ready to pick off
enemy aircraft

Every time I'd see a sailor
I'd point and ask my mother
Is that my dad? Is that my dad?

In my second year he came home
and the battles began
Running the house like a ship
white gloves over the surfaces
beds to be made without a wrinkle
Beatings to be had
if you pee your pants
even if it's his first day home
even if you are only two
and whatever he wore
it was a wife beater
a child beater
from a long line of
child beaters

child deprecators
child mockers
child silencers

Decades later, on Christmas
he would apologize
for being a bit rough on me
and, barely touching his shoulder
I would say
It's all been forgiven long ago
as a tear rolled down his cheek

Forty-five years in factories
and then two decades volunteering at the hospital
making off with the leftover sandwiches
to give to the birds
always with an angle
Quick to get an appointment
with the right doctor
when needed
always with an angle

Beaten as much as beating
he looked after my mother
during the first two years of her dementia
cleaning up after her, lifting her
but by the end of it
he too was beginning to fall

Just as she heads off to extended care
the lockdown hits
and he's left alone, still self-reliant
for almost two years
well-liked

much assisted by
the neighbours
his shoulders perfecting
their question mark curve
The house kept shipshape
until at 92, eyes start to go
and he can no longer drive
Then appetite goes
and he begins to shrink
and the daily walks stop
deep circles under his eyes
a cadaverish look
Locking the door
checking the door
locking the door again
insecure
uncertain

till he also must go
into what they call *care*
still in mid-lockdown
COVID picking off the nurses
the staff withering about him
tempers short
His distaste for brown bread
his insistence on white bread
The weight still falling away from him
the nurses, the doctors irritable
talking sharply
offending his pride
his dignity
They don't know who he is
the seas he sailed
the ports he patrolled

Some are kind of course
but some bring tears to his eyes
when they berate him

He is afraid now
as I was afraid of the dark
He wants the door to his room left open
as I did
His bladder is broken
he pees himself
as I did
embarrassed
more and more weight dropping away

A barren room but for
a flat-screen television
the remote almost impossible for him to operate
the skin hanging loose
from the once well-muscled arms
star-shaped welts and bruises
like bullet wounds
where the IVs went in

I retrieve that photo
from the now-empty house
and place it on the dresser
beside the TV

When the nurse comes in
she sees it
Who is that? a sunny Caribbean accent asks
That's my dad, I answer with a smile
My, my, you were a sailor, she says to him dotingly

My father stares fiercely back from the picture frame
the white sailor's cap
still haloed around the young man's head
his eyes still on the sky
Yes, I say with a little pride
Seven years in the British Navy

Oarsman

Sail on, my father
what a silly walker the world has lost
what a deafening emitter of raspberries
what that doodlebug missed when it missed you

You saw London burning from your front door
you heard the sirens screaming
you sailed through the Pillars of Hercules
to Aqaba and back
your photo anchoring the home shelf
over two small boys who waited

No one could row a boat
like you
accurate, even, parting
the Trent River precisely
in long, widening vees
V for victory, for the geese overhead
and sunfish below

You placed me atop the piano
so I could loose my two-year-old song
at a work party
my first show
my first applause
you strode to the bully's house
and the bully never threw a stone
at my head again

Everything was money
or so you said
until those last two decades
volunteering at the hospital

You were stingy when we were poor
when I held the ladder as you painted
the high eaves
but you came from poverty
from hunger
to get your wage's worth
feeding the famished families of Easter
turning them loose on the all-you-can-eat
like locusts on a granary
What a worker the world has lost
what a nicker of goods
The Earth hanging from your grip
like a piddling pup
as even to your last breath
you held
the hand of the mothership

There are sandwiches
hidden in places
behind the stars
for your pilfering
to feed the birds
and beasts of eternity's backyard

and the dogs are with you
Sally, Rocky … striding the sky beside you
never letting loose a bark or a sniff
at the God you didn't believe in

But you were real
you were, you *are* my father
You took your time
knowing it would require years
for things to come around right
but things came around right
Now you sail on
priestless Priest
Big Ed
the prow of your vessel
heading to that promontory
where a man can turn and watch and wait

Your hand only empty
a while
your hand a country
a house
a weapon
steady at the oars
every stroke
moving you beyond

every stroke
widening
in the world
you leave behind

The Yellow House

For years I stayed away from the yellow house
There were key-shaped shadows in corners there
that opened wounds
Where I accidentally turned off the last light
and screamed for hours
terrified of the dog's eyes
Walls where a meal hurled in rage
hung and slid
Counters where a man choked a woman
The bathtub with its would-be ring of blood
Places where I had prayed anyway
The window where I waited
and watched her leave
saying she'd never return
Good hidings
Palace of perpetual denigration
anxiety central
shrieks of a beaten dog
forbidden to speak
Where he leapt over the length of the table
pounding down on me
Right! Out of this house in two weeks!
rarely to return

And now all the old furniture
turfed out
the knick-knacks dispersed
father in ashes
mother in care
strangers examine those old rooms
walking through ghosts of agonies past

judging the wallpaper
noticing stains
fixing prices in their heads
and soon it will be sold
and I want to return

Places where I played
That bedroom closet
where I first learned the harmonica
The bedroom where my mother
snuck in pieces of bread at night
when we were hungry
That front door where my father
first brought in the dog
hidden in his jacket
The bed where I wrote my first poem
All that light pouring in the massive front window
The shared wall where we blew our horns
loud as we could at the neighbours and laughed and laughed
Eggs we threw in winter at the backyard neighbour's windows
frozen yellow
and now I want to go back
I need some ritual
I need to let the yellow house be
I need to let it go
but I want to hold it there
in a new sun
do it over
make it happy
these ghosts freed to the sky
this hall I'll never walk again
this door forever shut to me

The Day After the End of the World

I'll see you on the day
after the end
of the world
and I will be your honoured son
and you my faultless father

When all this flailing
and crying out is done
in that peace
of nothingness
we will show the feelings
we could never show
tears of joy mingling
in the glory of reunion

In that time after
the end of time
we will be family again
all anger spent
the agony of dying dissipated
You and my mother
will face up to your love
then turn to us
your children
love beaming
unguarded, full on

as we sit down to a table
where all are perfect

Micropoems II

Disconnect ion

Apeakoilypse now

The sweet herenow

Meritocrats

Inadvertisements

Respect for fact sayers

Justice has been swerved

Fulfilment not fillfullment

T(wang)

Cataclitoris

Lefteousness

Demautocracy

Psychopathogens

Don't breathe the despair-air!

Swipe

It is easy to erase the email
with a plea to follow some friend on Spotify
Swipe left and a little red panel with the word *trash* in it opens
Bye-bye
Even easier for the person whose name is vaguely familiar
wanting donations for her Indiegogo campaign. *Swipe*
I continue down the list of new arrivals
weeding out the unwanteds
quickly and efficiently but
I almost close my eyes and turn away
when I get to the subject line reading
Factory farming's next victim
same thing with
Save Puffins from Extinction
For a microsecond I pause
then open the panel, swipe, and proceed

No problem erasing connection requests
for LinkedIn or Poem of the Day
but my pace quickens
with the email
that asks for donations toward
food and water
for the latest souls
being herded
and ethnically cleansed
I can't, I won't
erase the updates
on the wars in Yemen
and the Sahara

These are my chosen causes
I have given before and will again but
there are women in Iran
I won't be able to help
I cannot donate to cancer research

swipe
I can't give to victims of the earthquake in Turkey
breathe in, breathe out
swipe

I tell myself, pick your battles
I tell myself, you can't save everyone
I tell myself
I do what I can
I tell myself
it is unproductive to feel guilty

The Side I'm On

I'm on the side
of the little kid who can't stop shaking
the side of the mother who just got the phone call
that said run, evacuate
I'm on the side of the young man
just stepping into the crosshairs
the woman being raped
I'm on the side of the old man
coughing up smoke
I'm on the side of babies in daycare
in a target-rich neighbourhood
I'm on the side of noncombatants
the ones taken captive
those vomiting with fear
I stand with
those who lost their legs
with the infant suckling
at a mother who is no more
I'm on the side of the boy
who wanted to be a poet
the girl who wanted to be a doctor
I stand with those hiding and praying
I stand with those trying to quiet
their children
trying to quiet their own hearts
people in the way
burning
I stand among those who have not strangled
their empathy
I'm on the side of the woman
trapped in the rubble

the ones the bullet
just missed
the one ten bullets
danced to death
I side with those who see no way out
no way in
those who are the last
of their family
the young of Yemen
the terrified in Sudan
those who pray for deliverance
in Colombia
I'm on the side of
the one digging
her nails into her palms
the one whose cries of *no*
have never been heard
the old woman who has forgotten
and the young man who can't stop remembering
the ones who dared march for human rights
the ones who didn't succumb to hate
the ones who refused to obey orders
the ones who couldn't pull the trigger
I'm on the side of those
seeking shelter
those who are not senseless with rage
I'm on the side of those who won't kill
the boy gasping in his own blood
the people trapped between war machines
those under heat-seeking missiles
I'm on the side of the evaporated
of the tortured
I'm on the side of those crammed in
of those who spoke out

I'm on the side of those whose sons and daughters
are sent out to slaughter or be slaughtered
the side of those whose nation
is no more
those for whom there's never been a home
the ones used as messages
the infant halfway through the alphabet song
I'm on the side of those
who haven't been talked out of compassion
of those whose deaths fill a quota
of those whose voices I'll never hear
of those on their way to a mass grave
of those whose deaths are part of an estimated number
I stand for the nonviolent
for those who were just going to the market
for those who just happened to be in the wrong place
for those whose grief can only grow
those who will never even vaguely know justice
of any kind
I stand with the plague ridden
those who bear no insignia or uniform
I stand with those whose village is just now being circled on a map
those whose names won't make it
to casualty lists or newspapers or tombstones
I stand with the thirsty
the children of Yemen
the women of Afghanistan and Iran
the hunted of Burma
the famished of Eritrea
the vanished of Canada
those in unmarked graves
I'm on the side of the lost
the blinded
the impoverished

the disappeared
those whose land has been stolen
the scapegoated Other
I stand with the hopeless
and the hopeful
with the ones who sang for peace on Earth
and the one who sang
Everywhere is war

Hunger from a Drone
(Gaza, February 29, 2024)

A small grey rectangle
the aid truck arrives

Iron filings converge upon a magnet
ants swarming a dropped chocolate

They may have weapons
hidden in their skeletal hands
Their hunger may be explosive

Hard to tell
from so great a height
if assault rifles
have gone off

A last meal
of high calibre bullets

Hunger lying arms
outspread
twig thin

The looks on the faces
of the killers and the killed

Too far below
to register
against the rubble

Curse on a Warmonger

All these perforated bodies drained of final agony
so you can cast your murder cloak wider
so you can stride
a red carpet of young men's blood
to clutch your hideous prize

Vengeance makes me want protracted death for you
but there's no time for that
Die quick and soon and take your rapists with you
Fall now and may the ground rush up to meet you

May the nation's blood you bloat with
thicken fast and choke you
May that cloak of burning blood leap up off the land
and smother the cabal of cronies who sip the red smile
from your trickle-down lips
May all that took burning months to destroy
recoil in a blistered instance
upon their venal flesh and all that was agony
collapse into their dying last gasp

Quick at drone speed fall upon yourself
dragging those blood-drunk flies
far underearth
forever deep and defunct
Now — before another bleeding second drains the clock
of unnumbered children's blood
A miraculous new instantaneity
A weapon-melting quickness
The only thing faster than light
your dying

Hate Takes You Back

Hate takes you back
when all have disowned you
When you rot in disgrace
there is still a place for you

Hate takes you back
like a long-lost mother
hate is waiting there
like a holy place

Hate takes you back
when heaven has rejected you
when the state has cut you loose
when your last hope
evaporates
and the rich and the poor
have turned away
and left you to your fate
there is still one who waits
dark and magnetic
at the final gate

Remember this face, amnesiac?
Hate, hate takes you back

Insurrection Day

Turn the bigot magnet on, unleash the storm
From all across the states, let them be drawn
the riff-raff rabble, dupes, the disinformed
aroused to insurrection by the con
Come raise that pop-up gallows to the sky
Attack! There's hardly anyone on guard
Come, peasants, wave those pitchfork flags on high
Don't worry, you'll be pardoned if you're charged

They smash down windows, swarm the sacred walls
and beat police. They've planned well for this day
Some smear with shit their names on hallowed halls
and hunt like rapists their divided prey
who hide in fear and yell in common cause
Tell Trump to stop them! frantic cell phones in their paws

We Burn More People

We burn more people than ever
We are the greatest incinerators in history
We turn little children into bonfires
Their mothers are at once their mothers
and their own funeral pyres
We incinerate whole families
at weddings
burning brides

the youngest of the sacrificed
never knowing
as they're running burning
that they're bringing democracy
to the Middle East

Twelve Things I Learned from My Research

There is a glass ceiling beyond the glass ceiling
and a glass ceiling beyond the glass ceiling beyond that

The stars are exit wounds
the stripes stripped directly from slavery's back

The energy used to electrocute murderers
is generated by burning Iraqi children

They are dustbowling the aquifer

There are GMO wheatfields growing thin golden guns
and bullets that sprout from corncobs

There are more and more babies on death row
in privatized prisons

They've replaced the wolves with themselves

There is a plan to make razor blade bannisters

You can't be anything you want to be

The silver lining in every cloud is mercury and the rain is hard

The house itself is an un-American activity

The light at the end of the tunnel
is a nuclear explosion

What Happened to the Ark

A world was ending
but we couldn't escape
There was nowhere else
We couldn't detach ourselves from the sky
the river
We were part of the lake
it had our shape

We were burnt into one another
inseparable
unable to be alone
only able to kill ourselves in others

I would've decried the injustice
I was part of
but I despised the language

Everything that illuminated us
was built on burning oil
molten metal
We were soldered into the stars
We tried to tear them away, but we wound up
stripping off our own flesh

and then when winter came
we had to burn the ark to keep warm

The Promise of Peace

If I could be the water
when peace is cracked and dry
If I could be a sheltering place
when peace is cast aside

Even when my table's full
and I sit before the feast
may I always keep a place in my heart
for the promise of peace

If I could be a feather
when peace is trying to fly
If I could be a single step
when peace needs to climb high

Even when I'm locked in doubt
and I fear there's no release
may I always keep a place in my heart
for the promise of peace

We must be the sunshine
when peace is lost and dark
and we must be the bread of love
when peace is cold and starved

Even in the threat of war
though hopes shall fade or cease
may we always keep a place in our hearts
for the promise of peace

If I can be the smallest breeze
when peace is stalled at sea
If I must lay my anger down
then let me take a knee
If I love this tired Earth
and its child, humanity

May I always keep a place in my heart
for the promise of peace

May I always keep a place in my heart
for the promise of peace

Micropoems III

If bridges must be burnt, it is best to cross them first

The blessing of distance is the curse of the local

The highway likes it both ways at once

Forever is only an estimate

Is the space between us expanding or are we just getting farther apart

Don't burn your bridges at both ends

Evolution thrives on bad copy

When you count your lucky stars, be careful not to burn your fingers

The present is the end of time as it evolves, infiniternity at the event horizon and consciousness its surfer

Every single moment is unprecedented

Every single person is a minority

There's always enough time for everything else to happen

The closer we get to the speed of light, the more I love you

There is forever in everything

It Won't Fit into Poetry

It won't fit into poetry
what I have to say

The words slide off
they don't dig in

Language just bursts
and hangs in tatters

its wrists blown out
its head bashed in by back-handers

It's so big you can hardly even talk
around it without stretching it so thin

It snaps and lashes back
python-like to strike you

It would be better to just look at one another
and nod knowingly

It would be better
not to even try to say

Poetry Expects

Poetry expects
Shakespeare
it expects Natalie Diaz
It stands there by the desk
with its jaw locked
eyes boring through me
like points of nails
just after the hammer hits

Poetry expects me to say something
to take a stand, a position
to hold up my hand with all its flab
melted away to elegant essence

It expects me to veer always to the difficult
let fear be the compass
to point the way
to where I'm unsure, unclear
and forget the cost
forget the allegiances
to anything but truth

Poetry expects the prolific
with no attachment
only ruthless oversight
little darlings strewn
in its wake

Poetry demands the miracle
be repeated and repeated
the hat full of rabbits
and winged horses
in up to the armpit
going after wisdom
and always trim

It wants me to be immortal
just so I can keep writing it forever

Poetry has no mental health days
if I'm sick find the verse in a lung full of phlegm

It yanks me out of bed
and throws me up against the morning sky
Look! Listen! it says
There's something there
even when there's nothing there

For Your Eyes Only

I have written this only for you
Please do not reveal its contents

Let's just say that silence is a secret we're gonna keep
and, if anyone asks, you never read it

You got to here
and stopped

What we all want from this poem
is deniability

None of us read it
none of us recited it
and certainly — none of us wrote it

Nuts dropping on keyboards, over time
over many seasons
beneath an oak tree
wrote this

We won't be mentioning it again

None of us has anything to fear
if all of us are dishonest

Clock at Midnight

The long last-second marathon
is in mid-career

on the very brink
of tomorrow

Before whatever calibrates
the absolute instant to change the date

changes this date
weary final increments

must wait
reluctant on the scaffold

unready for their fate
Beneath them like grand dames

their mother hours
rattle and prate

praying for an end to sorrow
When will the pardon come?

But alas the clock is struck
The last second drops

and the day is done
Murdered some would say

throttled as it's torn
from the arms of its child

the first moment
of the new morn

Apple

A marvel
the way you reach 'round
yourself in all directions
and tuck in at the top
tight to the stem
seamless
October's plump bough bender
borne to Earth
by the weight of its own sugar
an unbreached Jericho
safe in its skin perimeter

You are in our cheeks our eyes
our hands full of russet-wrapped medicine
perfectly packageable apple
with your palm-shaping curves
piled up in pyramids
squared and cornered
bred for boxes
cloned, copied
baskets of self
of stars in a red house
with your myriad memories of thorn
and your one rose mother
pith, pulp, pit, juice, and flesh
all of it a loss leader
for pollen's polygamy

It was Eve who tossed
your taste of disobedience
at Newton's head
Eve who left you waiting, one bite gone
by Turing's deathbed
You stretch our pockets
bob away from our teeth
Everywhere we go
we seek the apple
and find the world
Everywhere we reach
we reach for the apple
and come away
with hands full
of sun

Potato

Hey proletarian earth apple
always with the moon tentacles
your flesh luminous, numinous
your kiss yellow
purple, white
every shard fertile
clone worthy

Hey proletarian earth apple
always with the moon tentacles
your flesh luminous, numinous
your kiss yellow
purple, white
every shard fertile
clone worthy

Hey under-earth Shiva
trailing incipient potato ellipses
we claw, we dig, we scour
we peel
to do your bidding

You are shovel's purpose
famine's answer

Your reach Earth-wide
pulls us all in
to your thin-skinned embrace

the taste of aquifer
of well
of stone you can eat

Inside the Onion

I

The onion is poetry
that makes you cry
It would be hilarious
if there was a potato inside the onion
but there is always only another onion
inside the onion

II

Concentric
skins
translucent
a satellite of selves
temple inside temple
inside temple
ecosphere
bathysphere
atmosphere
seeking
that luminous last inner onion self
the quantum
indivisible
unlocatable
mirth onion
full of moon

Papaya

Sun's canteen
in green fatigues
plump with pulp
soft orange sun flesh

One smooth cut
and mirror images
fall away from each other
contraband black pearls
exposed
teeming with tomorrow
a gourmet grenade
that goes off slow
on the tongue

A taste
of what's at the heart
of light's appetite for light

The Weed That Grows Wild

The weed that grows wild
that you can't stomp out
green leaf, purple buds

The weed that gets you talking
laughing
Presence weed, fabulizing weed
Washington's weed
that makes a great shirt

Weed you can't ignore
growing on the path so aromatic
That weed you had once in Ireland
in Honolulu
Good writing weed, mood indica
the blue-budded, pain-easing herb
its grey threads pulled in from burning embers

Coughing weed
to exfoliate the lungs
to stop the spinning
to stop the vomiting
that grows up everywhere wind-born
tough spirited
the flower's flower of power
sticky on the fingers

Community weed that binds the many
in one smoke, one secret

Weed whose seed we eat for protein
that bees feed on
Skunk weed you smell on your clothes for days
gusts puffing up from the breast pocket

Weed so pretty you hate to break a bud
Strange prayer weed you hardly dare smoke
that frightens you
enlightens you

Earth weed in exile

Paraquatted, burned in heaps
weed that puts a man away for years

Sacred weed with will of air and fire
popping up like truth
like the hydra
wanting to get into people's heads

Poem weed
kept in a box by the bed
Dark comedy marijuana,
Good music-listening herbage
widening you
for all harmonies

Good sex sativa that makes your flesh
a sponge to bliss, to friction
to fiction
Good tongue weed that heightens
all tastes because
it makes a mind out of your mouth

At-long-last weed after a day's work
Lost flowertops you still hunt for
obsessively even years later
A twin to the molecule of bliss

The best
streaming weed, radiating from all fingers
all eyes
with outlaw grace
These purple rays
these beams of smoke
that toll
the long green gongs
of goddesses in us

Micropoems IV

If you give a dog a banana it will eat for a day
    but if you teach a dog to pick bananas you are a fool

No matter how you put a poem on a plate it will never be a fish

A monkey is a search engine

Couldn't a camel just go around a needle eye?

Many ointments actually require a fly

Make love like the dog's not watching

Partial fools do yoga to become complete fools

If you can keep it in it's simply not a laugh

What part of *yes* don't we understand?

Bitterness loves the taste of itself

We live in an unparalleled universe — it's all intersections

When the fire gets so hot it melts the melting pot

Of all our abilities, it is our gullibility that is most relied upon

If All Words Were Rose

If all words were rose
what would we say?

Language helps us
differentiate

It is in our interest
to go by the rules

Though whose rules
is hard to say

A rose by every other name
is a dictionary

a monotonous red lexicon
that only smells like language

Key

Your jagged edge
cut to match
its negative
a hollowed out
doppelganger
immovable without
you in it

every mountain
edged into
every valley
exact

a metal code
completing you
long enough
to turn the Earth
into its unreachable
inner self
— and open

Guitar Heroics

Slung about the hips
slashed sideways
with a windmill arm
spirit volts
jolt loose
from the axe groove
of flaunted lust
a come-on machine
pulsing song into
every crevice
of skin or sky

Let the humbucker buck
against the grid
Triplet those dyads
Rev those wheels
in rock and roll mud
and squeal out so hard
the nuclear string sings
its old abandoned nation-wide wire
stretched across the high ends of Earth
pole to pole

Bow the latitudes
Let the longitudes resound
Bend the parallels
into one another
two at a time
Burning bottlenecked
riffs slide
into our bottom-most beings

the players and the played
made one

The world lost
and found
in sound

like sun rolling down
sheet metal highways
dragging stars behind

Prince Pantoum

There's joy in repetition, Prince sings
So come on, let's play that cut again
Check out his lips when he bends the strings
Once more fresh ink fills the poet's pen

So come on let's play that cut again
Maybe we can dance the age away
Check out his lips when he bends the strings
Couples twerk or simply grope and sway

Maybe we can dance the age away
curlicues of ink across a page
Couples twerk or simply grope and sway
Thermals, panthers cycle in their cage

Curlicues of ink across a page
check out his lips when he bends the strings
Thermals, panthers cycle in their cage
There's joy in repetition, Prince sings

Because I Don't Forgive Brown Sugar or Some Girls

Time is on Jagger's back
It stalks his face
like if the Mona Lisa
had a hate child
with a shattered clay pot
vinyl groove tree rings
deep round his eyes

The last time I saw him
he was on the run
all over the stage
like something was after him

Poor death
It stalks his heels
unaware
it won't be satisfied
He's made a deal
with music
to be undying

Like Sybil though
he keeps ageing

Unstoppable lips and a pair of eyes
in a sheet full of wrinkles
nothing can iron out

Micropoems V

Self-consciousness is a form of absence

Self-esteem is not a democracy

Sometimes I feel like a matterless child

I'm trying to find the other half of the indivisible world

I thought I was embracing the darkness but when I awoke it was myself I had in my arms

I'm close to finding a cure for longing
(I've never wanted anything as badly as this)

I'm so prophetic I get pre-traumatic stress disorder

I'm so far out I have to pull the envelope

I know one word that says everything

I believe in the afterlove

I'm having a long-distance relationship with myself

I can count the world on one finger

We are accidents after happening

I believe in life after birth

We are vain in vain

If there were a cure for wickedness, would you be willing to take it?

We are what we do with what is done to us

We are wealthy only when everyone has their fair share

The justice system is like a hockey rink — it can only achieve its goals on a level playing field

Wearing trousers begins at home

There's more than one way to get fur on your face

All words are followed by invisible question marks?

If I'm not completing my sentences lately

A Where Ness

a where ness
a when ness
a why ness
a who ness
a what ness
a will ness
a will der ness

a wit ness

Mr. Joe

Remembering
all the love you gruffly gave
that great foot making the Earth
keep the beat
shaking the house with song
taking twilight out of the sky
fastening it a night at a time
to whatever you choose
as canvas
gentle with the brush
but blunt with fools
your wicked laugh
as you paint some Earth-defiling liar's face
in asshole caricature

Too bad to lose the pain
you have to lose the whole world
and Karen too
your voice broken
your hands too shaky
for brush or guitar
but death can't have all of you
your voice, those elegant riffs
in vinyl grooves
a sky more beautiful
than sky can ever be

The same sky that pressed down
that bound you
powerless to do anything
but take yourself

out of it
a hole in the air where you disappeared
a Joe-shaped hole
of a man flying
free again
threading the needle
shaking off
the Parkinson's
like an outgrown cloak
shaking off the shakes
an absence bigger
even than your giant frame

It won't take much to make me think of you
a forest made beautiful by dawn
breasts, bikes, birdwings anywhere
but twilight most of all
to gaze up into that indigo
so often pulled down through
your brush
in beauty I'd have missed but for you

Look, it's an M. Joe sky

Ten-four

Where Is Peter
(for Peter Lafferty)

I call his name to canyon walls
and no echo returns

I call his name outside his house
no answer comes

I knock on the door
no opening

no Peter stars
in laughing eyes

In bars and halls
a silent space
where music used to be

the generous hand
stilled so young
the guitar like an abandoned heart
leaning against the wall

Kate without a father now
Sarah bereft

We'll never sing

"Don't Let Me Down"
in harmony again

fucking cancer

I thrash my own guitar
uselessly

my bad timing
outlasts his patience
his beauty

that great voice
smooth as streams
rough as rocks
no longer sings

The Neighbourhood Is Not the Same

Swallows are missing
something from the centre of their song

Wind is just wind
It's not a way

If there are trials
they are not quests

Pain, strength, wit is wasted on them
nothing will complete you

That is not play
the children are merely moving

Where lovers wait
no romance

only biology
The hills are debunked

The heart is but a pump
the soul mere neurology

My voice is missing
something

notes, melody, and a name
I can hardly bear to say

Elegy for Masami

If there is a way
may it open easy to you
If there are endings
may the pain end first
If there is a journey
may your love go with you
and yet remain
Let your energy continue
in the good things you did here
Let the child in you once more
know homecoming and mother love

If you are extinguished
may there yet be fire that flickers
at the mention of your name
May your ashes nurture Earth
lift high again the new Yoshino leaves
May your DNA dance on
in the steps of your descendants

If there is an afterlife
let there be chess in that place
If you are complete, let there be
a space inside you
and a space beside you for another
May you travel in the grace of your own forgiveness
and your care still flow out from you to solace
May the grief at your departure
find a measured place in those you leave behind
May they know all that ever was
ever will be

May your flame leap in the centre of the sun
May goodbye never be forever
May hello again be always ready at our lips

Many Elegies

Too many elegies this year
some deaths may have to go unsung
or there'll be no time
to write birth poems
poems celebrating poplar trees

And still we lose each other
amidst the breaking out
of beauty

What if while mourning life
we missed the miracle
What if in chiselling runes into tombstones
we missed our children's
first words

We will have to find a balance
between joy and mourning
between outrage and grief
between the poppy and the rose

Why Michael Rothenberg? I cry
Why Peter Lafferty?
Why Graeme Williamson?
Why Shirley Eickhart?
Why Jim McNamara?
Why my father?
Why Joe Mendelson?
Why David Baxter?
Why Pauline Shirt?

And already I've missed
what's happening with the clouds
the way they've shifted
to give up their rain

Why do we disappear?
Why do so many go at once?
Even if a hundred thousand blades of grass
bend before my window
to the mesh and complexity
of sunlight
sorrow has me

I know one day
I will have to give up the grief
relinquish my protest
against the inevitable
but right now, I support the impossible
Right now, I continue
sailing the funeral barge armadas
back toward life
on streams of tears
I do not weep alone

Space Where Michael Was

Space where Michael was
what can ever fill you again?
The world leaks out
the wind howls through
the needle eye
threadless

Place where Michael stood
where will we find such gravity
What will hold the Earth down now?

Warmth where Michael was
what will wrap 'round Terri now?

Your clothes your hat
empty as our hearts

Every morning
we wake to the old world
where you live on
and then that world
is cruelly gone

Love that Michael once was
our love still leans in there

Death howls enraged
it has your hands, your heart
but a voice still shouts and sings

Our tears cannot fill the void
cannot float you up to us again alive
but here's to the undying
the poems death can't touch
the poems that burn death's cold hands

One Hundred Thousand Poets
(For Michael Rothenberg and Terri Carrion)

A hundred thousand stars
break over the world
Someone so forever
has gone

We face one another from all directions
weeping
a hundred thousand tears
A hundred thousand medical documents
feed the fire
A hundred thousand winds bear away the useless smoke
but that voice lives
It leaps the flames, transcends the page
Bad medicine didn't stop it
this voice that drew us in
brought us face to face
language to language
he and his beloved
centring a wheel
with a hundred thousand spokes
to turn against the stilled will of the world

We're drawn from around the globe to you
many threads pulled into one cloth
a garment for change
texts meshing with texts
one page affecting another

But now having organized the bards
you are called to the infinite

to align the stars
in constellations of change
leaving at our centre
a beloved space
sacred with absence

How dare death take you so soon
the ancestors weep
the future mourns
your beloved Terri weeps and burns
How dare grief
swell so many throats
wring so many hands

Those lungs that took in life
and bellowed out poetry
that turned air into love
how dare they fail you
feeding rivers and oceans
with tears
we would have turned into hallelujahs

You will not be forgotten
my brother
the Earth will not be silent
about what you have done
In us you continue
a hundred thousand memories
guard and amplify what you have left

The words that shook Salerno
will shout even louder against
the deadlock, the gridlocks
of injustice

In us the will to change
lives on
your name lives on
grief the fuel for all we have yet to do

Always Almost

If as Einstein says
everything that ever was
ever is
what is goodbye?

We pass through time
always almost present

Eternally we say
goodbye
But goodbye
is never forever

We move only forward
along the curve
We say *see you later*
not as wish but as prophecy

What the infinite created once
eternally recurs
Chance that made us
makes us all by chance again

The wave that carries us
from what we were
into what we'll be
will be again
Lovers weeping
mothers crying
fathers dying
part in vain

Goodbye has hardly left our lips
before those other words recur

Hello again

Micropoems VI

Most noise at night is caused by people trying to be quiet

There is no evidence that the creature who leaves no evidence ever existed

Faith is in the muscle memory

Live like the gods are watching

The forbidden fruit isn't the apple it's the peach — Hate's peach

The law is only broken when it's not upheld

People who can't thank you enough usually go on to thank you far too much

The language police have nothing left to say

Language is artificial intelligence and grammar is algorithm

Just because you find meaning in something doesn't mean it's a message

Mask communication

The closer and quieter the teacher speaks to you, the fouler the breath

Language has become a means of excommunication

Why keep de-meaning the language?

Go Get a Parachute and Fall

Go get a parachute and fall
in as much love as possible

Pillows, mattresses, duvets will be needed
to absorb the impact of the fallen

Why this talk of walking on clouds?

We fall through clouds
We fall through Earth

With just one look
time dissolves *up*

There is only down
into the depths of love

But the heart hits
no bottom

To plummet deeper
into love is all

fools want from
running hand in hand
at the precipice

Let's Not Wait

Let's not wait for misdirection or coincidence
We can't depend on cancelled flights
A ticket mix-up might never happen
I'm not going to rely on walking into the wrong house
at the right time
The chance of chance encounters
the probability of the improbable
the likeliness of the unlikely won't do

Leave happy accidents
for romantic comedies
Fortuitous typos
on misdelivered mail
are so statistically insignificant
as to be utterly discountable
It's not going to happen just because
everyone said it was impossible
I could miss you, you could miss me
Nothing is written in the stars
Let's be proactive
The odds are not with us
It's been 10,000 years
of the wrong stuff
We're not going to suddenly be placed
face-to-face
on some chessboard
We're not going to collide
at a crossroads
Let's not rely on a shipwreck
and a desert isle

Why wait
for the end of the world?

To Make It Happen

Enormous forces are at work
Nuclear power plants

printing presses, buses
even roses are in on it

cutting short their lives so you can sell them
on a corner I might walk by

Construction projects suddenly arise
Crowds collide and block certain routes

Far-off records skip
on songs I have to hear

drawing me two streets over
where roads that never met before

shift to intersect
There are new down-slopes

Everything tilts toward a valley
where bridges burn or not

depending on what love requires
It doesn't matter where

It might be in a daycare
might be in a crowd

our eyes first meet
But they do

and love that never was
immediately is and ever will be

Rash Wish

Think of me when you shouldn't
when you are at your hottest

Associate me with things incessant
Long for me like a thorn

If I could just be something
you prick your eyes open on

If I could only be the pen-tip
that scrawls whatever ink

there needs to be
to link us

to that system of signs, enough
to transmit one raw rough charge

Think of me
when you mustn't

Think of me when your wedding is at risk
Think of me when it's been a long time

Think of me once in a while
when you almost wish you could stop

but don't
because you can't

When We Make Love

Sometimes when we make love
we make more than love
We make art
We make ziggurats and pyramids
We invent fire when we make love
Without love
without sex
no flute, no lute
no saxophones

First we make love
then love makes us
and we make hooks and nets
What was the first step in the Great Wall of China?
Millions of people made whoopee
How did we get to Australia?
We made love, love made us, we made boats
and when we sailed and got there, we made more love
which made more of us who made boomerangs and didgeridoos
It was the groans and moans of coupling that gave us speech
It was sexual intercourse that begat Enheduanna and Gilgamesh
The first thing that had to occur for Einstein's miracle year — coitus
straight up-and-down missionary movements maybe
or maybe that particular insemination got wet with a little oral sex
Maybe it was oral sex that first opened the doors of poetry
Because of sex we made war, we made peace
The rosy engines, the regal pistons of copulation
gave us movable type and the printing press
Say *fuck* with the same mouth that says *miracle*
the same lips and tongue that shape the word *country*
Without fuck, there's no us

When the Goddess opened the box of the world
and took out the instructions
first thing on the list was
Make love

A Just Love

Desiring you
is good for the environment
Wanting you
is sustainable
I need no plastic
to go on loving you madly
Oil need not be scoured out of the aquifer
for me to hold you precious
I don't need nuclear power
to adore you
My love for you does not depend
on the incarceration of innocents
or the employment of the underaged
My love for you
kills no whales
No one gets burned alive

I don't need to pull down stars
No need to blaspheme the roses
because you are sexy
The waters are not poisoned
by my love
It will not stop the education of women
if I love you forever
My love requires no increase
in arms manufacture
No new dams, no new fracking

It cost us nothing to supply the dawn
with our thankful faces
We seek no awards, no medals
for the beauty we give to the world

I Love You Now

I love you now and now and now

I don't know for sure that I loved you before you were born
before I was born
or if I will love you in other lives
but I love you now

I see no end yet to the moments lined up
ready to happen, and I want to sing of the certainty
that my love will radiate through those moments
But what if I have a brain injury?
What if I am the first man to fall through the mantle of the Earth?
What if I am hit by a comet?

I definitely love you now
and the now keeps replacing itself
with always a new now
each one with me in it
constantly loving you
When you explode at me
when you get me wrong
when you misinterpret me
when you make a disappointed face
there I am loving you heartily

And when some small fault reveals itself
in that presence
my love for you lives
And when the angles and the light of your face
catch me unprepared and I am dazzled
by your physical beauty

I love you then
I love you when you are unjust
when you say the wrong thing
when you blurt out the right thing
I'm not sure I loved you with the face you had
before the world began
I can only say that I have heard you snoring
and I loved you then
I loved you when you were in pain
I loved you singing and preparing food

There is a strong likelihood
in whatever moments
tumble us into more and more moments
in each of those
I will love you then and then and then
just like I loved you when you were griping
just like I loved you when your moral nature was helpless to hide
when your honesty even to your own disadvantage
presented its truth in shaky voice
When you are brave, I love you
Even in brief moments of cowardice, I have loved you
in your eruptions, in your blossoming
in your longing
with all your bodily functions
and mine
in your constant rebellion
in your inexplicable stubbornness
when you don't say *good morning*
when you ask me if I like you
if I still love you
I continue to give that so-far answer
that 50-year-old answer
that nod of my head

I Believe

I believe the universe had no beginning
but then I see you and time starts again

I never desisted in my disobedience
until you said *hold me* and I did

I have no doubt all is sheer chance, chaos randominity
until you press your lips deliberately to mine

For sure the present is unattainable, unreachable
but then I spend long stretches in your arms

I considered myself a ruin, a failure, a sham
but I found you and my need was perfect

I am fragments, I am broken glass, a problem
solved, reassembled, made transparent by a caress

I was resigned to my selfishness
but gave myself to you completely

Nothing yet has cured me of atheism
more than your body against mine in the night

If I'm not spiritual
how can I want to love you forever?

I have no free will
until I know I have to turn my sail away

and go back into the wind
to where you wait

So Much Distance

So much distance when we're close
Your eyes skid away

We are north poles, each propelling the other
to a different room — a different commitment

Exhausted, overworked
you are called upon to save someone

and I've already been saved
In my dreams you are surly

I'm trying to get to you
I see you far away but then you're gone

You hit the bed flat out
your lips lost in a breathing machine

There's a little dog between us
Earbuds in my ears

I lie there wondering what I've done

Like a stranger in the shadows
on the far side of the street

your hand crosses over
into the other world

and slides warm into mine
our fingers interlocking

as you sigh

Micropoems VII

The new hadron collider — trying to get a teachable moment and a learnable moment to come together

My ability to incense meets your insensibility

Don't lean in so far you knock it over

Keep the open side up

While you're wasting your mind, who is minding your waste?

New promises for old! New promises for old!

Give me the serenity to change the things I cannot accept

Love: one burning moth circles another

When longing becomes belonging

If you can't take love, you can't make love

The heart is like a seed: it's got to break to grow

The only cure for the love that is the cure for love is love

Rapture loves company

The true act of rebellion against the regime of these times is to maintain friendships

There is no poetry in Hell, just poetics

Eat around the outside of the donut: what's left is poetry

Poetry changes everything — even nothing

By the time you tell the time the time has passed

We live in an unparalleled universe. (it's all intersections)

Baby Steps

My son and his wife and new baby are planning to visit
from Japan and will stay with us for some months

I'm nervous. Will he scorn my vocal exercises?
Will I still be able to sing my songs like no one's listening?

I can't blame him if he's not the biggest fan of my music
Probably it took up too much space in his childhood

All that practising, all that strumming and wailing
All the trips, the family holidays that were actually gigs

When he arrives, I give him a heads up about the exercises
how silly the scales and vowels might sound to him

but the first day as I begin to warble, he joins in
and I hear that he has a very flexible high voice of his own

His wife, Minako, also joins in and even the baby
and Marsha. It is fun and bonding

but that doesn't mean he likes my songs

Brimming with character, the baby is full of humour, curiosity
loud tyrannical demands and sweetness. Plus she seems to really like me

A man called Grampa!

She could already crawl when she arrived, but before her first birthday
teetering a bit, she proudly learns to stand

They take a little side trip to Chicago
and there she learns to walk!

When she returns, she is all over the place
pleased with her strides, her mimicry, her babble-talk

One morning she sounds a note and holds it steady: *AAAAh*
so I sing a harmony note over it and Marsha sings another

even higher note and soon
we are all joyously harmonizing along

To my surprise as my monthly gig approaches
I learn that my son and his family will attend

I'm still a bit uneasy. But all has been friendly so far
and the baby loves me. So I do my best to relax about it

In fact once on stage at the gig I lose self-consciousness. The band is great
and with a little shot of Glenlivet in me I'm singing well and really putting out

to lots of applause. Afterwards Minako tells me
I have a nice voice. Eli says nothing in particular and I don't pry

I've felt his scorn before and there is no scorn now
Besides, the baby has had a wonderful time

Nothing specific is said about my performance
in the car on the way home

I can handle that. I'm okay with myself
I leave them in the living room and go about my business

Later that evening though I discover that the baby
has learned yet another new skill

She stands up firmly when I re-enter the living room
and starts to clap her hands together smiling

Laughing with delight, we all applaud along with her
as I take a deep bow

Granddaughter

It took a while
after I first asked *shall I pick you up*
for you to say your word for *yes*

That was being chosen
that was getting a prize
to look so close into your eyes
The warmth of you
like the world itself

You were heavy
and I'm no Atlas
but I carried you where you pointed
always honoured
to be a horse, a camel, a walking tree

Soon we got so used to each other
you'd shout if I put you down
you'd cry if I left the room
Baba, Baba

If nature called
I had to hurry out
behind your back
and scoot up stairs
hoping you wouldn't notice

I think you liked my
little dances, my funny walks
my silly vocalizations

You'd mimic them
and all would laugh

Your requests to be lifted
once shy
once quiet semaphore
were now tyrannical, commanding, demanding

I might've grown strong
lifting you
or broken
Either way, I didn't disobey

though half the time I knew
your main purpose in my arms
was to see those higher places

to examine more closely
the bureau-topping tchotchkes

one of your few words, *baby*
always directing me
to another image of a baby on the wall

but then came coughing
COVID
and what I'd been unable to do
I had to steel myself to do —
refuse you

turn you down
let you rail
my face masked
I'm so sorry Grampa's sick

I felt like a traitor
but finally you sensed consensus
you stopped insisting
no new orders or directives emerged
you achieved acceptance

I cast little looks
my heart bereft
aching to hold you high at least once more
before the final days passed

but now it's time to leave
and COVID still with me
the plane set to carry you

so much higher
than my arms could ever reach
all the way to Tokyo

not one last hug
only a distant wave goodbye

continents, oceans
to keep us apart
until the next time

when you come with words
even heavier
and I lift you
if you let me

close to that place
in my heart
only for you

Halfway

I keep moving
halfway
to apocalypse
the increments so small
I can only take each moment
as it comes
time very slow

Signs shoot past me
the portents disappear
in the rearview mirror
I am overtaking bullets
missiles
I can actually see
light's progress
can dart in front of it
and not get caught

Halfway through a word
and halfway through
the next half
and halfway through that

I'll never finish
saying *I love you*

but I see you
and I run halfway to you
and halfway again
halfway again

You are right there
at the end of the world

Acknowledgements

Earlier versions of some of these poems have appeared previously in *The New Quarterly*, *First of the Month*, *Shot Glass*, *The Mocking Owl*, *Explorations in Media Ecology*, *Vallum*, *Dissent*, and on the CD *People Like You and Me*.

For their helpful comments on early drafts of some of these poems the author would like to thank Marsha Kirzner, Max Layton, Carolyn Smart, Susan Glickman, Karen Gut, Alison Stone, John Adames, Heather Ferguson, Maria Jacketti, Noelle Canin, Jaymz Bee, Allen Booth, Michael Rothenberg, and my editor for the past two and a half decades, Michael Holmes.

I would also like to thank the Arts councils of Ontario and Canada for their financial assistance over the years.

Special thanks to Pilar Rodriguez Aranda, Lorenzo Digianfelice, and Ben Cleveland.

Entertainment. Writing. Culture. ─────────────

ECW is a proudly independent, Canadian-owned book publisher. We know great writing can improve people's lives, and we're passionate about sharing original, exciting, and insightful writing across genres.

─────────────── **Thanks for reading along!**

We want our books not just to sustain our imaginations, but to help construct a healthier, more just world, and so we've become a certified B Corporation, meaning we meet a high standard of social and environmental responsibility — and we're going to keep aiming higher. We believe books can drive change, but the way we make them can too.

Certified
Corporation

Being a B Corp means that the act of publishing this book should be a force for good — for the planet, for our communities, and for the people that worked to make this book. For example, everyone who worked on this book was paid at least a living wage. You can learn more at the Ontario Living Wage Network.

This book is also available as a Global Certified Accessible™ (GCA) ebook. ECW Press's ebooks are screen reader friendly and are built to meet the needs of those who are unable to read standard print due to blindness, low vision, dyslexia, or a physical disability.

The interior of this book is printed on Sustana Opaque™, which is made from 30% recycled fibres and processed chlorine-free.

FSC
www.fsc.org
MIX
Paper | Supporting responsible forestry
FSC® C016245

ECW's office is situated on land that was the traditional territory of many nations, including the Wendat, the Anishinaabeg, Haudenosaunee, Chippewa, Métis, and current treaty holders the Mississaugas of the Credit. In the 1880s, the land was developed as part of a growing community around St. Matthew's Anglican and other churches. Starting in the 1950s, our neighbourhood was transformed by immigrants fleeing the Vietnam War and Chinese Canadians dispossessed by the building of Nathan Phillips Square and the subsequent rise in real estate value in other Chinatowns. We are grateful to those who cared for the land before us and are proud to be working amidst this mix of cultures.

ecwpress.com